The Red Sea and Persian Gulf

The Red Sea and Persian Gulf, nestling among the exotic countries of the Middle East, are two of the most important waterways in the world. The Persian Gulf and surrounding countries produce one-third of the world's oil; and in the Red Sea, thousands of ships plough their way to and fro, carrying valuable exports through the Suez Canal. In this book you will get an idea of the contrast between the new world and the old — the bustling modern ports and the traditional Arabic way of life. You will see some spectacular pictures of the coral reefs of the Red Sea and be shown some exotic and glittering fish which depend on the reefs for food. Take a look at some modern feats of engineering — not only oil platforms, but the Aswan High Dam and sophisticated desalination plants — which have helped transform parts of countries such as Saudi Arabia and Egypt from stifling hot, barren land into fertile farmland and thriving communities. A glossary and index are included.

SEAS AND OCEANS

The Red Sea and Persian Gulf

Edited by Pat Hargreaves

WAYLAND

SILVER BURDETT

© Copyright 1981 Wayland Publishers Ltd

First published in 1981 by
Wayland Publishers Ltd
49 Lansdowne Place, Hove,
East Sussex BN3 1HF, England.

ISBN 0 85340 770 3

Published in the United States by
Silver Burdett Company
Morristown, New Jersey
1981 printing
ISBN 0 382 06584 0

Phototypeset by
Direct Image Photosetting, Hove, Sussex.
Printed in Italy by
G. Canale & C.S.p.A., Turin.

Seas and Oceans

Three-quarters of the earth's surface is covered by sea. Each book in this series takes you on a cruise of a mighty ocean, telling you of its history, discovery and exploration, the people who live on its shores, and the animals and plants found in and around it.

The Atlantic
The Caribbean and Gulf of Mexico
The Mediterranean
The Antarctic
The Arctic
The Indian Ocean
The Red Sea and Persian Gulf
The Pacific

Contents

1 FIRST IMPRESSIONS

The long narrow Red Sea runs through the heart of the hot lands of the Middle East. It separates Egypt and the Sudan on the African side from Saudi Arabia. One of the reasons why it is called the Red Sea is because of minute plants which spread over the surface and give it a reddish colour.

Since the Suez Canal was opened in 1869, connecting the Red Sea to the Mediterranean, sea traffic has been able to travel directly from Europe to the Indian Ocean, avoiding the trip around Africa and so saving thousands of miles.

The Red Sea is bordered by many countries. Some, such as Saudi Arabia, are rich and powerful; others like Ethiopia and the Sudan are very poor. The climate of the region is very hot and dry, and much of the land is desert. Although the brilliant sun, warm blue water and numerous coral reefs make the Red Sea a paradise for divers, very strong winds can bring fine sand from the deserts on either side, and sometimes the air can be stiflingly hot and humid. There are few fertile areas where the people have found it possible to farm the land. Some work at local crafts while

Below The old and the new. A traditional Arab *dhow* contrasts strangely with this modern port scene.

Above Arab boys check their nets by the blue waters of the Persian Gulf.

others help to build the new towns. There are still nomadic tribesmen to be seen in the desert, travelling with their livestock from one fertile area to another.

To the east of the Red Sea, sandwiched between the other side of Saudi Arabia and the Zagros mountains of Iran, is the Persian Gulf (sometimes called the Arabian Gulf). The Gulf is very shallow — less than 100 metres (330 ft) deep and is filled with very thick deposits of sediment. Enormous fields

of oil and gas have accumulated in this sediment, making the Persian Gulf the most important source of these fuels in the world.

Imagine a visit to one of the countries on the western shores of the Red Sea — Egypt for example. In the north-east this country is bordered by the Gulf of Suez, and the Suez Canal. To the east is the Sinai Peninsula. The area to the west of the Gulf of Suez is very barren. In this desert roam the nomadic Bedouin tribesmen, who live in tents made of goatskin and rely on camels for transport. They make a strong contrast with the settled populations in the Nile valley and the bustling capital city, Cairo. On the outskirts of Cairo are the ancient pyramids and the Sphinx, which were built over 4000 years ago, and are a breathtaking sight. There are also more modern achievements to see, such as the Suez Canal and the Aswan High Dam.

Across the Red Sea from Egypt lies Saudi Arabia, the only country with coastlines on the Red Sea and the Persian Gulf. It is now one of the wealthiest countries in the world, mainly because of its rich oil resources. Saudi Arabia is also the home of Mecca, the holy city of the Muslim religion where the prophet Mohammed was born. Thousands of pilgrims visit the holy places there every year.

Oil from the Persian Gulf, on Saudi Arabia's eastern coastline, has brought employment for its people as well as wealth to the country. The money gained from oil exports has helped to build schools, hospitals and universities. The Gulf also provides other valuable resources such as fish and shrimps.

Other countries which border on the Persian Gulf also have oil reserves, and in countries such as Iran, Iraq, Kuwait, Oman, Qatar and the United Arab Emirates, this new-found wealth is also being used to bring more employment and better health to the people of the Gulf.

Right Map of the Red Sea and Persian Gulf.

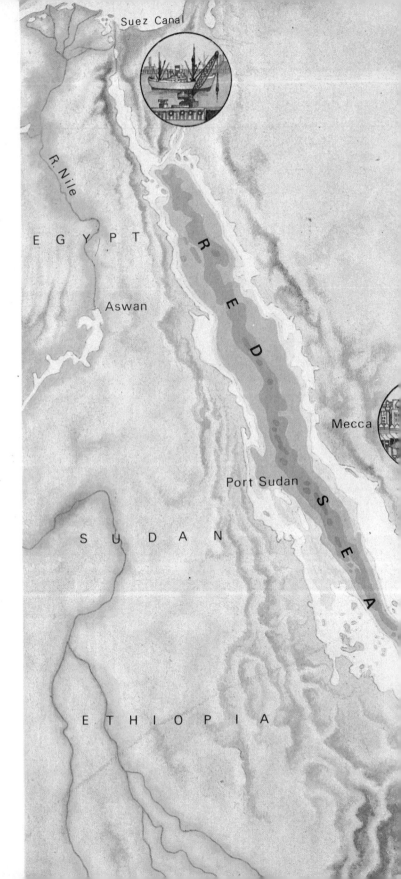

IRAQ

KUWAIT

I R A N

P E R S I A N

BAHRAIN

G U L F

Straits of Hormuz

GULF OF OMAN

AUDI

UNITED ARAB EMIRATES

O M A N

A R A B I A

INDIAN

YEMEN

SOUTH YEMEN

GULF OF ADEN

OCEAN

SOMALIA

2 THE MOVING LAND
How the Red Sea was formed

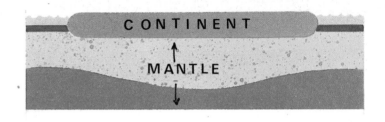

The surface of the earth is not still, but moves very slowly, a few centimetres every year. Sometimes continents break up and move apart, allowing new seas to form between them, or separate continents move towards each other, squeezing out the oceans between them.

The Red Sea was formed about 40 million years ago, when, what are now Saudi Arabia and its adjoining countries, broke away from Africa. This happened because movements deep in the earth pulled at the old continent, and stretched and thinned it. At last it broke completely in two, and molten rock, or lava, rose up from inside the earth to fill the gap, and hardened.

But hardened lava is heavier than many other types of rock and it did not fill the gap completely. It left a narrow trough, which was deep enough to be filled by the sea. In fact this trough has not completely filled with

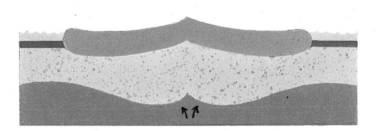

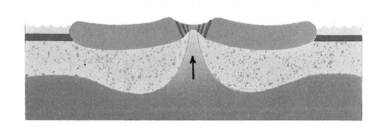

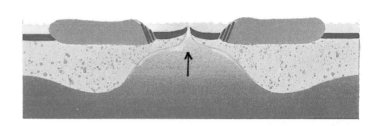

Right An upwelling of lava and molten rock from deep within the earth caused a continent, and part of the mantle beneath it to split. As the two parts of the continent (Africa and Arabia) moved away from each other, the trough in between flooded, and the Red Sea was formed. The Sea is slowly increasing in size as new rocks flow out from the mid-ocean ridge.

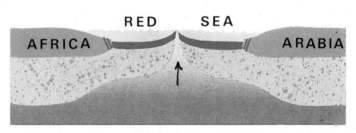

Right Artist's impression of the Red Sea and Persian Gulf drained of their water.

water. At the southern end of the Red Sea, in Ethiopia, the bottom of the trough is still above sea level. There we can actually see what happens as the 'sea' gets wider: new cracks form in the older lava, and new lava comes out of them. This cracking causes earthquakes, and the lava builds up into volcanoes.

The area round the Red Sea is one of the hottest places in the world, so the water evaporates fast. Usually the sea does not dry up, because other water comes in from the Gulf of Aden at its southern end. However, the channel is very narrow, and in the past it sometimes became blocked. Then the sea dried out, and left deposits of salt behind. In some places the salt is up to four kilometres (2.5 miles) thick. Nowadays, most of this salt has been covered by sediment.

There are valuable minerals on the bottom of the Red Sea. Sea-water can pass down the cracks which continue to form along its centre. The water is able to dissolve salt and certain minerals from the rocks, and it eventually carries them back to the sea bed.

There, the hot, salty water, which is heavier than normal sea-water, accumulates in pools on the sea floor. Eventually, the water cools down again and deposits the dissolved minerals on the bottom. In this way sediments containing large quantities of copper, nickel and other valuable metals have been laid down on the bottom of the Red Sea. These can now be mined.

Above Submersibles are used by scientists to explore the deep waters of the oceans, where divers cannot venture.

Right There are large salt deposits in the Red Sea.

The making of the Persian Gulf

Above This baby girl lost her home when an earthquake devastated her village in Iran.

Right Oil drilling platforms stretch as far as the eye can see off the coast of Bahrain.

The Red Sea was formed by a continent splitting apart. The Persian Gulf was formed as a result of two land masses — Arabia and Asia — colliding. Long ago there was an ocean dividing these continents, but it has shrunk to nothing, and all the rocks of its floor have been swallowed back into the earth.

Continental rocks (that is, rocks forming land masses), are lighter than the sea-bed rocks. They float on the earth's surface as part of a system of plates. Continental rock cannot be pushed down into the earth, so when two continents collide they bend and fold up. The collision between Arabia and Asia is causing the land in Iran and Afghanistan to fold, and high mountains are still forming there. There are also earthquakes, where the two continents are pushing against each other.

The collision has also caused the land masses to bend gently — even quite a long way from the edges of the colliding continents. One of these bends pushed part of Arabia below sea level, and the sea flooded it, forming the Persian Gulf.

Because it has been formed by a shallow bend in a continent, the floor of the Persian Gulf is quite different from that of the Red Sea. It is mainly composed of continental rocks like sandstone, and it is much shallower and smoother, with no cracks, earthquakes or volcanoes in it. Valuable minerals, such as oil, have been found beneath these continental rocks.

3 THE WEATHER AND THE WATER

If you were to visit the Red Sea and the Persian Gulf, you would find the climate hot. In some areas it is a little cooler in winter, but you would still need to shelter from the sun. In summer the air temperature can be as high as 40°C, very hot indeed. The sun warms the sea and you would find it pleasant for swimming.

There is very little rain over the land or the sea. On land it is difficult to grow crops. In many places there are vast deserts where only drought-resistant plants can grow. In some places there is irrigation and so crops can be grown. Sometimes the sea-water is made into fresh water by desalination, for example at Abu Dhabi.

Below Scientists take water samples at different depths to test for temperature and saltiness.

Above Water is scarce in many Arab countries. Wells have to be dug very deep into the earth to find a new supply.

The winds in most of the Red Sea and the Gulf blow mainly from the north or north-west. In the south the winds are more changeable. Here the monsoon winds blow mainly from the north-west in summer and from the south-east in winter. Sometimes, when the winds blow over the dry land, they create huge dust storms, making it difficult to see. Strong winds at sea make waves and move the surface water along, helping to form currents.

Winds also affect the temperature of the water. You can read more about currents on page 22.

When the sun heats the sea surface, some of the water evaporates and leaves salt behind. This mixes with the rest of the sea-water and helps to keep it salty. Very little fresh water enters these seas from rivers or as rain so there is almost no dilution of this salty sea-water. There is some mixing in the south with the slightly less salty water of the Gulf of Aden, but even so the Red Sea and the Persian Gulf remain two of the warmest and saltiest areas of sea-water in the world.

Scientists from many countries go to this region to collect water samples for testing. They lower special sampling bottles and electronic devices into the water near the surface and deep down. These instruments record temperature, salinity (saltiness), depth and other properties. In the Red Sea, near the surface, up to 39 parts of salt to 1000 parts of water has been recorded — a very high salt level. Beneath the surface, the water is even saltier. The surface temperature in the Red Sea can be as high as 32°C, but the deeper water is cooler. Scientists from the research ships *Discovery* and *Atlantis II* made a very exciting discovery a few years ago. They sampled the water at the surface and deep down and, as expected, the general pattern showed high temperature and salinity at the surface of the Red Sea and cooler, saltier water deep down. But, in addition, they found isolated pools of *hot*, salty water overlying the rocks of the sea floor at depths of more than 2000 metres (1.3 miles). This was a very unusual and exciting discovery because the temperature of these pools in the depths was about 60°C and the salt content was about five times as great as that at the surface. Although these pools are isolated patches it is thought that slow mixing with the surrounding water can take place. The extra heat and salt in these deep pools must have come from beneath the sea floor where salt deposits are found beneath the sediments in some parts of the Red Sea.

Temperature and salinity are important because they affect the density (heaviness) of the water. Warm water is lighter than cold water of the same salinity and so floats on top of it. Salt water is heavier than fresh water of the same temperature and will sink beneath it. The density plays a part in the circulation of the water between the surface and the deeper levels of the sea.

Right Much of the Red Sea and Persian Gulf is surrounded by hot, arid desert, where it is impossible to gain a living from the land.

4 THE RESTLESS WATER
Waves

Waves on the surface of the sea are caused by the wind. The Middle East is one of the less windy areas of the world, so it does not suffer from very bad weather or tropical storms. This does not mean, however, that it is always calm at sea. Sailing boats have plied these waters for thousands of years, and the waves can become steep and high enough to sink ships. In ancient times, winter was considered to be unsuitable for sea travel, but the boats used then were tiny by today's standards.

The waters of the Gulf are now dotted with oil-producing platforms. These structures must be designed to withstand the battering of the waves. The constant wear and tear of the water can cause metal fatigue which may make a platform collapse.

Waves not only affect the surface of the water, but also stir up the mud and sand on the sea-bed, up to 100 metres (330 ft) below the surface. Although wave *energy* can travel for thousands of miles, the water particles themselves travel hardly any distance. They move round in circles, travelling forward with the crest and returning almost to their starting position as the trough passes. When waves run into the shallows, they become a surge of water which rushes up the beach. If they approach at an angle to the shore, the ends of the waves nearest to the beach slow down most, with the result that they appear to turn, and march in formation straight on to the shore.

20

Left It is very unusual to see waves larger than these on this Red Sea beach.

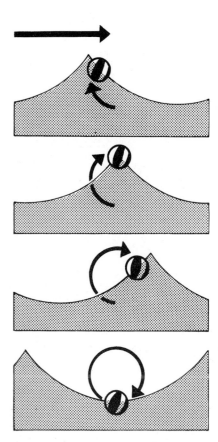

Above This beach ball returns to almost the same place, although it travels in a vertical circle with the passing of the wave.

Left Severe storms do occur, so oil platforms are designed to withstand the battering of the waves.

21

Currents

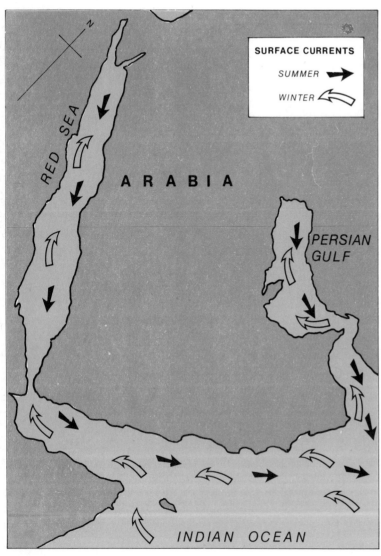

The Red Sea has an average depth of 524 metres (1730 ft), and a maximum depth of over 2900 metres (nearly 2 miles). In the north it is linked by the Suez Canal to the Mediterranean Sea. But the Canal is very narrow, making the Red Sea nearly land-locked at its northern end. To the south, water enters the Red Sea from the Gulf of Aden. The water movements are partly affected by the direction of the wind. In summer, there is a north-west wind, and warm, salty water at the surface flows towards the Gulf of Aden. In turn, cooler water with a slightly lower salinity, flows from the Gulf of Aden to the Red Sea. Because it is cooler than the surface water, it remains for a while beneath the surface.

In winter, the pattern of the water movements (currents) changes. The south-easterly wind pushes water from the Gulf of Aden to the Red Sea. This water is at first very warm, but as it goes further northwards it becomes cooler and eventually sinks and flows back to the Gulf of Aden. It is replaced by more warm, northerly-flowing surface water from the Gulf. In general, the level of the sea-water in the Red Sea, depends to a great extent, on the amount of water moved in and out by the currents. Water circulation caused by tides also has an effect (see page 24)

The Persian Gulf is much shallower than the Red Sea, with a maximum depth of only 100 metres (330 ft). A small amount of fresh water flows into the Gulf from the rivers

Above A simplified picture of the currents in the Red Sea and Persian Gulf. They depend mainly on the wind direction, which varies from winter to summer.

Above *Dhow* wharf at Bahrain. For hundreds of years Arab traders have used the winds and currents to transport their goods up and down the Gulf.

Tigris and Euphrates. However, the climate is so hot that often more water is lost by evaporation than is replaced by fresh water. To the south there is an exchange of water to and from the Arabian Sea at the Straits of Hormuz. As in the Red Sea, the direction of water currents in the Persian Gulf depends partly on the wind direction. For example, in winter the wind pushes warm surface water in a northerly direction from the Arabian Sea to the Persian Gulf. Gradually the water becomes cooler, sinks and flows back to the Arabian Sea. Look at the map to see the direction of the Red Sea currents.

23

Tides

Both the Red Sea and the Persian Gulf are almost totally enclosed by land, and both are connected to the main oceans of the world by narrow sea passages. The Red Sea is connected to the Gulf of Aden and the Indian Ocean through the Straits of Bab el Mandeb. The Persian Gulf connects with the Gulf of Oman and the Indian Ocean through the Straits of Hormuz. Because both seas are too small for the gravitational pull of the moon and sun to produce large tides within them, their tides depend on the ocean tides at the entrances. Strong tidal currents flow backwards and forwards through the entrances — in the Straight of Bab el Mandeb these reach speeds of one metre (3 ft) a second. The tidal range (that is, the difference in the depth of the water at high tide and low tide) at the southern and northern entrances to the Red Sea reaches about one metre (3 ft). But you would be wrong to suppose that the range is the same along the whole length. In the middle, around Port Sudan, the range is close to zero. To understand why this is so you could try a small experiment. Run about fifteen centimetres (6 in) of water into a bath. Now set the water in motion by pushing it towards one end and letting it swing backwards and forwards. You will find that the water has a natural rhythm, or period of oscillation, and although the water moves up and down at both ends, in the middle the level stays nearly constant. The tides in the Red Sea oscillate in a similar way, but on a much larger scale, with a rhythm of 12½ hours.

The Persian Gulf also has 12½ hour tides, but because it is much shallower than the Red Sea, its natural period of oscillation is longer, close to 25 hours. So, the Persian Gulf also has well developed tides with a one-day period in response to those tides in the Indian Ocean.

Right Low tide in the Persian Gulf. The tidal range is quite small in both the Red Sea and the Persian Gulf.

5 CORAL AND CORAL REEFS

The most spectacular and most beautiful of all underwater scenes in the Red Sea must be the coral reefs. There are few reefs in the Persian Gulf because corals do not survive well in the hotter, sandy conditions there. But the Red Sea is famous for its coral reefs.

Reefs can be thought of as underwater hills. Living corals cover much of the surface of these hills. They look like delicately coloured shrubs and bushes in an underwater garden.

Among the corals are many other small animals (invertebrates), and around and above the corals drift and swim thousands of fish of every shape and colour. The scene can be so dazzling, lit by the brilliant tropical sun, that it may seem to divers visiting the reef that they are swimming in a dream.

But what sort of animals are corals? You may have seen coral skeletons on sale in souvenir shops and not even realized that

Left The coral reef provides a rich feeding ground for these brightly coloured fish.

Below Many different types of coral grow together on the reef.

corals are animals. Corals in fact are closely related to sea anemones, such as the common red beadlet anemone found on rocky shores in Britain. Each anemone is shaped somewhat like a jar, with a single opening (the mouth), at the top, which is surrounded by a ring of tentacles. Each coral, however, consists of numerous anemone-like individuals joined together, side by side, to form a colony. Corals produce a large, limey skeleton. Most of the skeleton is secreted underneath them, so that the living animal ends up as a thin layer covering the surface of the skeleton. Each of the anemone-like members of the colony sits in a pore (a tiny hole) on the surface of the skeleton. If you look closely at the surface of a piece of coral these pores can be seen easily. However, in many types of coral the members of the colony are fairly small (perhaps 0.5 centimetres — a quarter of an inch — across, or smaller). Also, their tentacles may only be extended from the pores at night, when most corals feed. So you cannot always see the anemone-like individuals themselves.

On a Red Sea reef, there may be a hundred or more types of coral of various shapes. Many are branched like bushes or small trees. Many are solid and rounded, while others may be fan-shaped. It is the solid types in particular which build up the reef. When a colony dies, the skeleton is left and new colonies will settle and grow on top of it, until the reef reaches the surface of the sea.

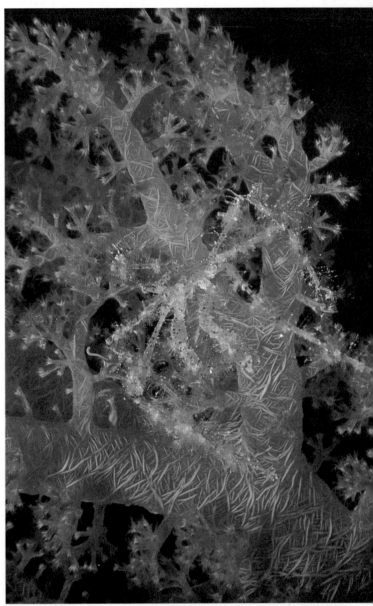

Above Some corals are soft and plantlike, such as this beautiful red variety.

Right A view of part of the coral atoll of Sanganeb from the top of the lighthouse which marks it. Many ships have been wrecked on such reefs in the past.

Several different types of coral reef occur in the Red Sea. Along much of the coastline of the northern and central parts of the Red Sea are well-developed 'fringing reefs'. These reefs are like elongated ridges running parallel to the shore perhaps several hundred metres away from the water's edge. Between the reef and shore is a shallow sandy lagoon, while most of the thriving corals and marine life are found on the outside of the reef. Often other reefs occur further out to sea, perhaps several kilometres away, rising up from deeper water. This type of reef is called a 'barrier reef'.

In several places around the Red Sea, groups of islands stretch fifty kilometres (30 miles) or more out to sea. Each island has its own fringing reef, and other isolated reefs occur between them.

Corals obtain some of their food by using their tentacles to catch tiny animals that come drifting past in the plankton. However, they make much of their food inside themselves. Numerous microscopic plant cells live within the coral itself, and these turn the energy of the sun's light into food. This situation, where individuals of one type of organism live closely with a quite different type, is not uncommon in the natural world, and is known as 'symbiosis' (meaning 'living together').

6 LIFE ON THE CORAL REEF
Coral reef animals

It is because of the corals that many other forms of life are able to find a home on the reef. They can use the holes and crevices formed by the coral growth to hide from larger animals which may threaten them. Some of these animals also feed on the corals. Others feed on the green seaweed (algae) which grows on the reef, and on plankton which floats past with the currents.

The variety of small invertebrate animals on the reef is enormous. They include sponges, shellfish, shrimps, crabs, worms of different types, sea slugs, starfish, sea urchins, sea cucumbers and featherstars. The most common sea urchin is *Diadema*, a large urchin with long, sharp, black spines, which feeds by scraping at the film of algae covering the rocks. In places there are so many that you have to take care while wading in the water not to tread on one.

Above Sea cucumber. These strange-looking creatures are eaten as a delicacy in some countries.

Left This crown-of-thorns starfish has poisonous spines. It can eat coral animals by turning its stomach inside out and attaching it to the corals.

Among the starfishes is the large crown-of-thorns starfish, which has ten to twenty arms and is covered with spines. This starfish feeds on coral, and is the same type which has done so much damage to parts of the Australian barrier reef.

The shellfish include cowries, spider conches and giant clams. The most common is the panther cowrie, which has a large, brownish mottled shell with black spots. The cowries feed, like the sea urchins, on algae, and so do the spider conches. The giant clams, which have two large saucer-shaped shells growing to well over thirty centimetres (about 1 ft) in diameter, feed by filtering the plankton out of the water. And the different species of cone shell, which have beautifully patterned shells, are predators which feed on worms and fish.

Among the crabs are several small types which are gaily coloured and live among the branches of the bush-like corals. If you peer

Above Sea slugs are one of the many small creatures that live on the reef.

Right This delicate creature is called a fanworm. When danger approaches, the whole structure will fold up and disappear.

into such a coral, you might well see two or more pairs of beady crab's eyes, mounted on little stalks staring back. These crabs feed on small particles of matter which settle on the corals. Often one or more solidly-built, pink shrimps, known as pistol shrimps, can be found living inside the coral too. These shrimps have one pair of pincers much larger than the other, and by snapping the pincers together they produce a cracking noise like the sound of a small pistol. This sound they apparently use to stun and capture small animals on which they feed. This is just one of a great variety of underwater noises which can be heard by the diver on a coral reef.

Scattered over the surfaces of many of the large, rounded corals you can see what look from a distance like numbers of tiny Christmas trees, each one a different colour — red or orange, yellow or blue. If you look more closely you can see that each tree is made up of a double spiral of small feather-like fans; then you may see the whole structure suddenly fold up and disappear into a little tube running into the coral. This tube is formed by a small worm, the coral fanworm, *Spirographis*, and its fans are its tentacles with which it breathes and catches food.

Fish of the reefs

The most obviously attractive animals found in these seas are the coloured fish which throng the coral reefs. Over a hundred different species may be seen within a few minutes on a typical Red Sea reef.

Perhaps the most attractive type of reef fish are the butterfly fish. They are ten to twelve centimetres (over 5 in) long, and are flattened from side to side, forming a thin, upright disc. From the front protrudes a small mouth. The sides of the fish are brilliantly patterned with yellow, white, black and other colours. The butterfly fish are nearly always seen in pairs, which occupy a home area or territory. The smaller butterfly fishes feed on the corals by picking at the tentacles, while the larger butterfly fish and the closely-related angel fish feed on sponges. In the Red Sea and Persian Gulf there are ten or so common species of butterfly fish, most of which are only found in that area. These include, for example, the little brown-faced butterfly which has an orange-brown head and a silver-grey body, and the large, blue-cheeked butterfly, which is lemon yellow except for a blue patch beneath each eye.

The most common of the reef fish are probably damsel fish. There are several different types, mostly about five centimetres (2 in) long. Along the edge of most reefs, dense shoals of damsel fish hover and feed in the water above the corals. Some are bright green, some grey, some black-and-white, some striped, and mixed with them are

Left A colourful swarm of fish in the Red Sea.

Above A clown fish swims above the waving tentacles of a sea anemone.

schools of a similar-looking but unrelated bright red fish called *Anthias*. The overall impression is of countless jewels dancing and sparkling in the water.

Two other common types of fish associated with coral reefs are the wrasses and the parrot fish. These two groups are closely related. Their bodies are brightly-patterned in green, orange, red and blue, and both groups swim by moving their pectoral fins up and down. (Pectoral fins are those on either side of the body, beneath the 'shoulder'). The wrasses vary enormously in size, from very small to the giant hump-headed wrasse, which may reach 1.75 metres (about 5 ft) long. But they all feed on invertebrates such as worms, shrimps and crabs. Most of the parrot fish are medium-sized and can be recognized by the way in which their teeth are fused to form a distinct parrot-like beak. This beak is used to scrape off the rocks the thin algal film which they eat.

Another important group of reef fish which feed on algae are surgeon fish. However, these have much more delicate mouths, and feed in areas where the algae is longer and can be plucked off the rock. Surgeon fish get their name from a pair of scalpel-like blades which stick out on either side of the base of the tail.

Finally, before we leave the reef fish, we should look at a few of the predators on the reef, which feed by hunting other fish. The

Below The lionfish is one of the more extraordinary fish to live on shallow coral reefs.

Above The grouper, with its wide mouth for swallowing prey, is the commonest predator of the reef.

most common and characteristic predators are perhaps the groupers. These are deep-bodied fish with large eyes, and mouths which are able to open very wide to suck in prey. Their bodies are usually mottled or blotched, mostly in shades of brown, but sometimes with red or blue. The very largest occasionally grow up to 2.5 metres (about 8 ft) in length, and are said to be able to swallow a human being in a single gulp!

The other common fish predators on the reef are the jacks. They are medium-sized fish with a streamlined form, flattened a little from side to side. In contrast with the groupers, the jacks spend more of their time away from the reef in the open water. They are coloured sea-grey, and so are well camouflaged. When hunting, however, they race along by the reef, often in groups of two or three, to take some smaller fish by surprise.

37

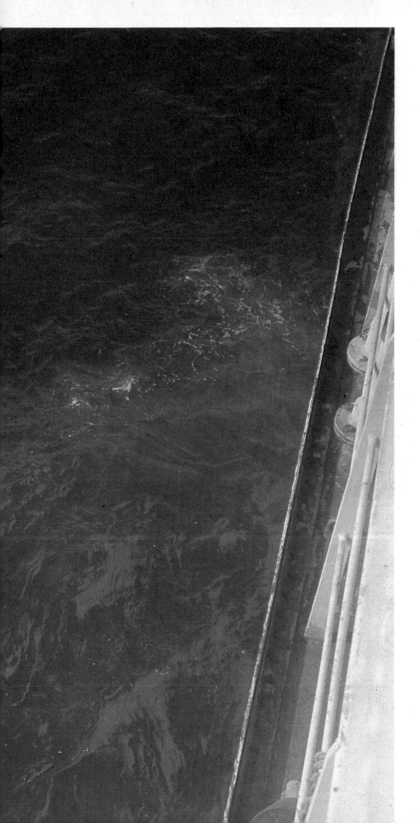

Life in the open sea

Apart from the coral reefs, these seas contain many other creatures of interest and beauty. Many of the smallest are found within the zooplankton, that is those tiny animals which drift in the upper waters of the sea. The plankton also includes huge numbers of microscopic plants — different sorts of algae each consisting of a single cell. One group however, called the diatoms, can usually be found as chains of cells. One diatom is of special interest because it contains an orange pigment. Sometimes it occurs in enormous numbers on the surface of the sea, and there is one suggestion that the red effect thus produced may be the origin of the name of the Red Sea. Many other types of sea plant have a green or yellow pigment.

The phytoplankton serve as food for the zooplankton. Most of these are microscopic, animals or small shrimps, but some, such as a variety of attractive jellyfish and crustaceans, are larger.

Left One tiny floating plant occurs in such numbers that it seems to colour the sea red — hence the name 'Red Sea'.

The very largest fish to be found in the Red Sea or Persian Gulf feed directly on the zooplankton. These are the whale-sharks, huge sharks reaching twelve metres (40 ft) in length but quite harmless. They have a hump-backed shape and are grey with large, white spots. Equally impressive is the largest of the rays, the manta ray, which also feeds on plankton. Rays are relatives of the sharks. They are flattened from top to bottom and have their sides drawn out into wing-like structures. The wings of the largest manta rays are nearly six metres (20 ft) across. The wings beat slowly up and down to drive the manta through the water with effortless grace, or sometimes they jump clear of the water in spectacular leaps as part of their courtship.

Below A huge manta ray 'flies' effortlessly through the water. The 'wings' of these creatures can grow up to 6 metres (20 ft) across.

High and dry on the islands

Various interesting animals and birds can be found on the many small islands in the Red Sea. These are desert islands, with almost no vegetation. Some, indeed, are covered with nothing but sand, while others have patches of low shrub.

Nesting on most of these islands are colonies of various species of tern, such as the white-cheeked tern and the lesser crested tern. All of these terns obtain their food from the surrounding sea — sardines and similar fish. On many islands there is often a pair of ospreys in residence. This is the same fish-eating eagle which has recently attracted attention by returning to nest in Scotland. Ospreys catch fish, such as surgeon fish and wrasses by grabbing them with their talons as they swoop low over the water.

Turtles too nest on these islands, especially the hawksbill turtle, which feeds on invertebrates on the reef. To nest, the adult females drag themselves out of the water and up the beach, where they dig a large hole and lay their eggs. They cover over the eggs before returning to the sea. Some weeks later the little turtles hatch out, dig their way out of the sand, and scurry down to the water.

Below A pair of ospreys have made their home on this desert island. They catch their prey by swooping low over the water and grabbing fish with their talons.

Above A turtle hatchling searches for food on the reef.

Animals of the tidal shore

Below the water's edge are a wide variety of habitats — muddy bottoms, sandy bottoms and coral reefs, mangrove swamps and seagrass beds. In these different areas many kinds of plants and animals can be found.

On either side of the Red Sea are a number of small creeks. These are called *mersas* on the African side, and *sharms* on the Arabian side. At the back of these creeks and in the large bays of the Red Sea and the Persian Gulf, fine sand and mud settles on the bottom. Although this mud is often short of oxygen many animals live in it. One such animal is a type of giant mussel. This is the large fan-shell *Pinna*. It can grow up to twenty-five centimetres (1 ft) long and lives with its open end sticking up out of the mud. On the surface of the mud lurk various crabs including *Lupa*, a large, blue, swimming crab which scuttles away with its pincers spread wide for defence if anyone approaches.

Mangrove trees are also found in these areas. There are many different types of mangroves, but they have all adapted to life in the salt water. They cope with the salt by excreting it through their leaves, while to deal with the lack of oxygen they have developed aerial roots. These roots may either stick up out of the mud, like spears set around the tree, or else they branch out from the lower part of

the tree. The thickets of mangrove in these areas are not as well developed as those found in other areas nearer the Equator.

Near the shoreline along most of the coast, the sea bed is covered with sand. Areas of shallow sea bed are often enclosed by the growth of coral reefs further out to sea so that a lagoon is formed. The sand here will consist of particles of broken down corals, other reef animals and plants. Within the sand live various animals, including several types of shellfish. Many of these, such as mussels and oysters, have two saucer-shaped plates or valves which are hinged together at one side. For this reason they are called bivalve shell-fish. These animals feed by means of a tube or siphon which reaches up to the surface of the sand so that food particles can be drawn in.

Also living in the sand are several types of sea urchin which have adapted to life in this area. They are flattened and disc-shaped with short, stubbly spines which enable them to move more easily through the sand. Because of their shape these urchins are known as sand dollars.

Some areas of sandy bottom develop dense beds of sea grass. Sea grasses are not sea-weed (algae) but true flowering plants similar to those found on land. In the shelter of these grasses are small animals, including various types of shrimp. These areas are important as the home of the young of the type of shrimp which is fished commercially in the Persian Gulf (see page 58).

Above An octopus searches for prey in this sandy creek.

Left A huge variety of animals lurk among the roots of these mangrove trees.

8 WATER AND ENGINEERING
The Nile and the Aswan High Dam

There has always been a special concern for water in the Middle Eastern countries bordering the Red Sea and Persian Gulf, because *fresh* surface water (that found in lakes, ponds and rivers) is scarce. One of the largest rivers in the region is the Nile, which has always been regarded as an important, even sacred river — the lifeline of Egypt. It provides water for drinking and water to irrigate farms.

Farmers have used many methods of lifting water from the Nile to their fields. Some ancient contraptions, such as the *shaduf*, are still used today. This has a pole with a bucket on one end for lowering into the water, and a counterweight at the other, which helps raise the bucket. As the population has grown, however (there are now 40 million people in Egypt), so has the need for water. Modern engineering has had to come to the rescue.

Dams and barrages (low, wide dams) were constructed in the 1840s, chiefly in the delta area north of Cairo, to provide farms with a regular supply of water over a wider area. Another group were built between 1902 and 1925, but by the 1950s Egypt was so short of water (and food) that something had to be done.

The first Aswan Dam was built in 1902. Work on the Aswan High Dam was started in 1958, and by 1964 the first water had been

Above Arab labourers at work on the Aswan High Dam.

Right The Aswan High Dam as it looks today.

impounded. The dam wall is 245 metres (810 ft) high and 3.2 kilometres (2 miles) wide. Trapped behind it is a huge reservoir over 105 metres (347 ft) deep, called Lake Nasser, after a former President of Egypt. (It is called Lake Nubia in the Sudan.) The 'lake' is over 500 kilometres (310 miles) long, covering an area of 6,000 square kilometres (2,200 square miles). It holds enough water to supply Egypt with all her needs for ten years. The scheme does not only supply water, it also stops the floods which used to devastate the towns and farmlands. Moreover, it provides hydro-electric power for industry, commerce and homes.

The Aswan High Dam has added nearly one-third more farming land to the 6.5 million feddans (*1 feddan* — 0.42 hectares) which were already cultivated in the delta and valley areas. Much of this new farmland is to the west of the Nile Valley itself, in an area called the 'New Valley' — a series of wide oases in the desert. Each square kilometre of farm-land in Egypt has to provide food for about 1450 people, so the new dam is vital to the people's livelihood.

Manufactured water

Qatar, one of the smallest of the Gulf States, has in the last thirty years become very rich, because of the large oil and gas deposits found off its shores. Until the 1960s there were few farms as we know them, and then only in the northern part of the country. Water would be obtained from wells, but because this water rested on top of heavier salty water, the supply in many areas was quickly exhausted as farms developed to cope with a new demand for food for an increasing population.

There are about 150,000 people in Qatar, mostly in the capital, Doha. Many of these have come from other Gulf States, and even Pakistan, to work on the oil and gas installations and the new farms. Since 1956, most of the people of Qatar have had their drinking water made available by 'desalination', an expensive process by which fresh water is manufactured from sea-water. Money from the oil and gas works has paid for the necessary factories.

One problem, however, is that the unwanted salt is released back into the coastal waters, with the result that the triangle of sea between Qatar, Bahrain and Saudi Arabia is far too salty for marine life to survive in it. As fishing is still important in this area, something will have to be done to stop this unusual sort of pollution. You can read more about desalination on page 54.

Below This complicated system of pipes is a desalination plant.

Right Vital water for irrigating the fields is pumped from a well on a government farm.

The Suez Canal

Perhaps the greatest engineering achievement in the Middle East is still the Suez Canal, designed by a Frenchman, Ferdinand de Lesseps, and built at the fantastic cost (even by today's standards) of £28 million. The Canal was opened in 1869, but the costs of construction and maintenance were so great, that eventually the British Suez Canal Company took over the running of the Canal. In 1956 the Canal was nationalized by the Egyptian Government.

The Canal is really a series of man-made

Left and above Two views of the Suez Canal. The Canal is still a vital link between Europe and the East.

water channels which link together a number of natural stretches of water, two of which are called the Bitter Lakes because of their brackishness. The whole length of water, from the Mediterranean Sea to the Red Sea is about 500 kilometres (310 miles), about the same as Lake Nasser.

In 1975, the Canal was reopened after being closed as a result of a war in 1967. Since then, the Canal has been dredged, cleaned, deepened and widened, so that today it can take ships of up to 100,000 tonnes. Eighty vessels each day can sail through the Canal in three convoys, two southbound and one northbound.

The Canal was built to save time (and hence, money) for ships travelling between Asia, Australia and Europe. Previously, the shipping route was by way of the Cape of Good Hope. The Canal saved over half the original time and cut fuel costs by nearly three-quarters, so that it was, and continues to be, a vital link between those continents. Not only that, the money paid by ships using the Canal is a very important source of income for the Egyptian Government and people — many of whom work to maintain the Canal system in good order, so that it will continue to benefit everyone.

Above A specially constructed pier for loading oil into supertankers at Kuwait.

Where it is found

The countries around the Persian Gulf produce one-third of the world's oil. They use only a small part of it themselves, so much of it is exported to Europe, the U.S.A. and Japan. It is shipped in large supertankers, carrying up to half a million tonnes of 'crude' oil each.

This oil is then refined and made into petrol, paraffin, lubricating oil, plastics and medicines. Without it, all industrial countries would soon be in trouble, because they would not have enough fuel for aircraft, cars and factories.

When oil is extracted from under the ground, large amounts of gas often come up with it. In the past this was usually burned in big flares and therefore wasted. This was because it was difficult to take it to other countries where it was needed.

Now, much of it is converted into Liquified Natural Gas (L.N.G.) by cooling it to a very low temperature (much colder than ice). As a liquid it takes up much less space than as a gas. It can then be shipped in special refrigerated tankers. When it is unloaded, it is heated up to air temperature and used like North Sea Gas in heaters and cookers.

Oil and gas started forming many millions of years ago, when dead marine animals and plants dropped into the soft beds of the oceans. Deep layers of these remains gradually built up over the centuries. Later upheavals of the earth's surface often forced

Above A tanker for transporting Liquified Natural Gas.

these layers thousands of metres below the sea bed. As the animals decomposed, they formed oil and gas.

This oil and gas was lighter than the surrounding water which was also trapped in the silt, sand or porous rock, and they would try to float to the surface. Some succeeded and evaporated into the air leaving a deposit of bitumen (a tar deposit), or formed food for marine animals. Other oil and gas became trapped in underground reservoirs, under solid rock layers which they could not get through.

If these reservoirs are big enough they are called oil or gas 'fields', depending on which resource is most plentiful.

Extracting oil and gas

We can now look at the way that oil is 'produced' from a steel platform on a typical undersea oil field in the Persian Gulf.

This reservoir holds 100 million tonnes of oil and lies three kilometres (nearly 2 miles) below the sea bed. The depth of the sea at this point is about thirty metres (100 ft). The largest part of the platform is the lattice tower which is held in place on the sea bed by long tubes (piles) which are hammered into the rock to stop the tower moving in a storm. Above sea level, out of reach of the highest waves, is the deck. This supports the production equipment and the accommodation for the forty workers looking after it.

The men work twelve-hour shifts around

Below Not all of the gas which is extracted with the oil can be utilized. Here it is being burned as a flare above the oil rig.

Right An engineer checks pipes at an oil terminal in Bahrain.

the clock for fourteen days at a time, before going ashore for a week's holiday. They travel in a helicopter which also brings out the replacement crew.

The oil comes to the deck through twenty wells. These are steel tubes, three kilometres (1.8 miles) long, lining the holes drilled through the rock above the reservoir. As in most oil fields, there is at first sufficient gas pressure to force the oil to the deck. As the oil is extracted, the pressure drops and the supply to the surface slows down or stops.

To prevent this happening the production equipment includes a number of pumps. Some of these pump water or gas down into the reservoir to keep the pressure high. Others pump the oil to the shore through a pipeline on the sea bed. Before it goes ashore, other equipment separates the water and gas from the oil. If there is only a small amount of gas it will be burnt in a flare on the platform. Otherwise, that too will be piped ashore.

Below Pollution is a big problem in an area which produces so much oil. Here an oil spillage from a tanker pollutes seaweed on a beach.

Above Irrigating sun-baked fields in Iran.

Right Women do much of the heavy work in water-hungry Oman.

Mineral resources

Apart from the oil drilled from the sea bed, the sea itself has both living and non-living resources to offer. Perhaps the most important of the non-living resources is the water itself, for in the countries around the Red Sea and Persian Gulf, fresh water is very scarce. Fresh water is needed not only for drinking, but for industry and for irrigation. Therefore, in an increasing number of places, fresh water is being obtained from sea water. This is done by heating the sea-water so that about half of it evaporates, forming water vapour. This is then piped into other vessels where it condenses into fresh water. The salt is left behind in the remaining original salt water which is now piped back into the sea. The whole process is called 'desalination', and is carried out in large desalination plants, which look like small oil refineries and are situated on the coast. However, because so much fuel is required to heat the sea-water, this process is likely to be economically worthwhile only in countries which have plenty of oil like Saudi Arabia..

Whereas sea-water can only be used if the salt is removed, the salt itself may also be valuable. Before the days of refrigerators, salt used to be very important for preserving food. Salt is also an essential element of the diet of man and his animals. In many inland areas it does not occur naturally. In the past, salt used to be collected from the coast in places where

Left In the hot lands of the Middle East, water channelled into pools evaporates fast, leaving large deposits of salt behind.

Above Sedimentary rock, like this lump, can contain all sorts of valuable minerals.

shallow pools of sea water had dried out. Sometimes parts of the lagoon along the coast would be filled by the higher water level in winter, and would dry out in the summer sun leaving a thick crust of salt. Camel trains would come long distances to load up the salt and carry it to inland markets. Today, however, salt production is carried out in a more controlled way. Large, shallow, artificial pans are dug beside the shore and filled with sea water which is left to evaporate in the hot sun. When most of the water has evaporated, the salt crystals are scooped out and left to dry out completely.

Most recently, another source of minerals has been found in the Red Sea. As we saw on page 18, in the very deepest pockets of the Red Sea, the water and mud is hotter and saltier than normal sea-water and also contains very large amounts of valuable metals, such as copper, zinc, tin, nickel and mercury. By pumping up the mud through long pipelines to a processing plant on a ship, it has proved possible to extract these metals. Unfortunately, however, some of the metals, which are poisonous, may be present in the waste material returned to the sea and these may harm some of the marine life.

The fishing industry

Above A quayside fish market in Oman.

Although the Red Sea may have poisonous minerals in it, it still contains large numbers of fish. More than 150 types of edible fish have been counted, and there are plenty of shrimps. We know that this sea contains nutrients, for there are often so many tiny planktonic plants that they change the surface colour of the sea.

Some of the fish here swim in the deep water, but most live along the continental shelf. This is the ledge which extends from the coast offshore, and is covered by a shallow layer of water. It is difficult for light to reach into deeper water, and as plants need light to survive, there tends to be less food for fish in these murky depths. Many fish live in lagoons and on coral reefs along the shore. Saudi Arabia has about 1600 kilometres (1000 miles) of continental shelf, compared with Egypt, the Sudan and Ethiopia on the west bank, which each have about 500 kilometres (312 miles).

Prawns, or tropical shrimps, are big business in Saudi Arabia, where 11,000 tonnes are landed each year. They are not so important in the other states, though Iran and Kuwait each catch about 3000 tonnes a year. The best fishing grounds are to the south of the Red Sea where the water is shallow. An important fish here is the barred Spanish mackerel.

Fish are mostly caught by hand fishing lines or gill nets (which trap the fish by catching their gills), and in net traps set along the shore. The shrimps are caught by towing a fine mesh trawl net behind a motor trawler. As boats become bigger and more powerful, the trawling method is also being used to catch fish. The boats most often used are the *huris*, a kind of canoe; the *sambuk*, which is about fifteen to twenty metres (50 to 66 ft) long; and the *dhow* which is a little longer and often has an engine.

British fishing experts have been helping Saudi Arabia to increase her catch in the Red Sea and the Persian Gulf. At present, this country catches 31,000 tonnes a year, compared to Egypt's 96,000 tonnes and Yemen's 133,000 tonnes.

In the Persian Gulf there is an important fishing port at Jubail. From here, about 100 *dhows* fish among the nearby coral islands. At Manifa, there is a fleet of modern prawn trawlers, and machinery for making ice. This is very important in hot countries, for fish soon go bad if they are not kept frozen.

The countries around the Red Sea and Persian Gulf supply much of the world's oil. They are now becoming very rich and able to spend money on better boats, ice-making plants and foreign aid. Unfortunately, many fishermen find they can earn more money ashore in the new factories, or building modern towns, and so they are leaving the industry.

Above Fishing nets are hung up to dry in the sun. Notice the traditional Arab *dhow* in the background.

Pearls and other exotic exports

Apart from fish and shrimps, there are other animal products which are taken from the sea. Most prized must be pearls, which are produced by the pearl oyster, *Pinctada*, a type similar to the edible oyster. A pearl is made when a grain of dirt finds its way into the inner part of the oyster. To protect itself, the oyster secretes layers of a fine, lustrous, shell-like material around the dirt. This material, called mother-of-pearl, is also found in many types of shellfish (including oysters) as a lining to their shells. The pearl oyster is found growing in shallow, sandy bays in the Gulf and the Red Sea, and the pearls from this area are famous for their quality. Today, large quantities of pearls are cultured artificially in Japan and the Far East, and the pearl fishery in the Red Sea and Persian Gulf is less important.

However, there is still a large demand for mother-of-pearl, which is used to make shiny shirt buttons and similar decorations. The most important producer of mother-of-pearl is the *Trochus*, a conical shell two to five centimetres (1 to 2 in) tall, which is found in large numbers, scattered about the coral reefs. These are fished for by native fishermen, who travel long distances in a traditional arab boat called a *sambuk*. When they reach a suitable area of reefs the men separate into small dugout canoes, called *huris*, in which they paddle over the reef top looking for the shells.

The curious sea cucumbers also occur on the reefs. They are collected by fishermen in *sambuks* and *huris*. Sea cucumbers are thick,

rough-skinned animals, shaped like large sausages, and related to starfishes and sea urchins. They lie about in shallow water where they eat food particles within the sand. They don't need to hide because they have few natural predators. Most people would not

Below A pearl diver surfaces with his catch of oysters. Notice the clip on his nose.

Above Pearl divers in the Persian Gulf. These divers work together in pairs, each one remaining below the surface for 60 to 80 seconds.

think them edible, but in Japan and China they are considered a delicacy, and they are exported to the Far East.

Above An Arab farm boy uses his camel to collect firewood.

A visit to Bahrain

The Bahrain archipelago is a small group of islands situated in the Persian Gulf. They are mostly of limestone rock and are covered with sand dunes. Bahrain itself is the largest of the islands, and is about fifty kilometres (30 miles) long and about twelve kilometres (8 miles) wide. The capital is Manama, which lies to the north. Two islands which are linked to Bahrain are Muharraq to the north-east and Sitra to the east. There are also numerous other islands, some of which are uninhabited. The northern part of Bahrain, quite near the coast, is cultivated, and you can see bananas, pomegranates, date palms and other fruits. In the central and southern regions the land is desert-like, but there are still plants which grow in the dry conditions. Although the climate is hot in July and August with temperatures which may exceed 33°C, it is cooler between January and March. Generally rainfall does not exceed about five centimetres (2 in) a year. You might see some wildlife: numerous birds, including the cormorant, diving into the sea for fish, and also jerboas, lizards, gazelle and camels.

Bahrain has an interesting history. It is thought to have been inhabited for thousands of years. On the island there are ancient burial mounds, remains of flint tools used by early civilizations, and other items of archaeological interest. The present people of Bahrain are thought to be of Arab descent but

Above Ships being unloaded at Bahrain's new port of Mina Sulman.

there are also people from India, Pakistan and other countries. Bahrain has always been a seafaring country. It used to be a great centre for the pearl industry, although recently this has been less important.

Since the 1930s there have been many projects which have helped to modernize Bahrain. A causeway now links Manama with the island of Muharraq, and a new port was developed near Jufair during the 1960s. This port, which is called Mina Sulman, provides harbour facilities for large ships such as tankers, liners and the large local dhows. Nearby, on reclaimed land, are slipways, repair facilities and storage areas. Another terminal on Sitra island is used mainly by tankers transporting oil products.

Many of the activities of the islanders are still associated with the sea. Coral is collected and used as building material and the traditional fishing industries still thrive. Also of importance is the boat-building trade. Boats built include the straight-keeled *jalibut*, the square-sterned *sambuk* and the *baghala*, which has windows in the stern and is rather like the old European man-of-war.

Port Sudan

Above This square-sterned *dhow* seems to have a problem with its rudder.

Approaching Port Sudan from the sea, perhaps in a cargo ship or a yacht, your first thought might be of the numerous coral reefs, where ships are sometimes wrecked. Some reefs are fifty kilometres or more (about 30 miles) out to sea, and those on the edge of the sea route leading into the port are marked by light beacons or lighthouses. For example, on the well-known coral atoll of Sanganeb, about twenty-five kilometres (15 miles) north-east of Port Sudan, stands a tall lighthouse. Ships coming from this direction need to pass this safely before turning in towards land.

Port Sudan was built at the beginning of this century on one of the natural creeks on the Red Sea coast. Before this the creek was named after Sheikh Bargout, a Muslim holy man whose tomb, decorated with flags, lies on the right-hand side of the entrance to the harbour. Beyond this the main quay stretches away in an almost straight line towards the end of the creek. A dozen or more cargo ships will be alongside the quay, being loaded and unloaded by tall cranes. Much of the cargo being loaded consists of bales of white cotton, the main export of the Sudan. To the left of the harbour entrance is a large grain storage silo next to which one or two more ships may be moored. Around the docks are many of the Sudanese — tall, handsome, people, most of whom wear long white gowns and white turbans. Some of the dockers have short jackets, short baggy trousers and long, tightly curled hair. They are from the local *Beja* tribe.

Behind the harbour entrance lies the town centre with large, impressive stone buildings housing the local government offices, the banks and the shipping companies. Beyond this is the *souk*, the Arab market, noisy and crowded with people buying vegetables and other foods, clothes and ironmongery from stalls and small shops. Around this are blocks of flats and bungalows, and further out the wooden chalets of the less well off. The town is expanding so fast, that on the edge of it, people who have recently moved in from the hills and desert, still live in their attractive tents made of camelskin and goatskin.

No visit to Port Sudan would be complete without a tour of Suakin, the old town nearby, which is full of houses built in the old Arab style, and which was the main port until Port Sudan was built. In fact, Suakin was an important port for hundreds of years, and in the fifteenth century a visitor described it as having more ships than any port in Europe. But so thick was the coral growth that large, modern ships could not enter the harbour, and so Port Sudan was built.

Below Herds of goats in front of the old town of Soukin, Port Sudan.

Glossary

Algae   Seaweed and other similar plants.

Barnacle   A small shellfish which clings to rocks and the bottoms of ships.

Carnivore   An animal which eats other animals. A shark is a carnivore.

Condense   To change from a gas or a vapour into a liquid.

Container Ships   Fast cargo boats which carry their goods packed in large containers rather than loose.

Continental Drift   The movement of the landmasses of the world towards or away from each other.

Continental Shelf   That part of a continent which lies offshore and is covered by a shallow layer of water.

Coral   Stony, skeletal structure formed in masses by simple marine animals (polyps). It is found in various colours and sometimes builds up into coral reefs.

Crustacean   Animal (usually living in the sea) with a hard shell and many legs. Prawns, crabs and lobsters are all crustaceans.

Current   The flow of water in any given direction.

Desalination   The removal of salt from seawater so that it can be used for irrigation and domestic purposes.

Evaporation   The changing of water into a vapour.

Invertebrate   An animal which does not have a backbone.

Irrigation   Watering agricultural land by diverting rivers or by building dams, reservoirs or canals.

Oscillation   Movement to and fro like a pendulum.

Plankton   Tiny animals (zooplankton) and plants (phytoplankton) which drift in millions through the seas.

Pollution   Contamination of sea-water by dangerous chemicals from industry, oil spillage and sewage or other rubbish. Parts of the Red Sea are polluted by excess salt pumped back into the sea after *desalination*.

Salinity   Saltiness. The salinity of sea-water varies a little according to the depth of the water, its temperature and its distance from the Poles.

Sediments   Clay, sand and silt which collects on the sea floor and may become hard rocks. Remains of dead animals are also incorporated into the sediments.

Souk   The market place in an Arab town.

Symbiosis   Where two organisms live attached to one another with mutual advantages.

Tides   The rise and fall of sea level which usually occurs twice a day because of the attraction of the sun and the moon.

Books to read

Adam, Robert E., *Oceans of the World* (National Book Co.)

Angel, M. and H., *Ocean Life* (Octopus Books)

Clemons, Elisabeth, *Waves, tides and currents* (A. E. Knopf)

Cochrane, J., *The Amazing World of the Sea* (Angus & Robertson)

Cook, Susannah, *Closer look at Oceans* (F. Watts)

Engel, Leonard, *The Sea* (Time, Life)

Fair, Ruth H., *Shell collectors guide* (C. E. Tuttle)

Gaskell, Thomas F., *The World beneath the Oceans* (Doubleday)

Howard, George, *How we find out about the sea* (Transatlantic)

Keeling, C. H., *Under the Sea* (F. Watts)

Lambert, D., *The Oceans* (Ward Lock)

Merret, N., *The How and Why Wonder Book of the Deep Sea* (Transworld)

Parsons, J., *Oceans* (MacDonald Educationals and Silver Burdett)

Read, Richard, *The living sea* (Penguin)

Ryan, Peter, *The Ocean World* (Penguin)

Saunders, G. D., *Spotters' Guide to Seashells* (Usborne)

Stonehouse, B., *The Living World of the Sea* (Hamlyn)

The people who wrote this book

Pat Hargreaves   Marine biologist, Institute of Oceanographic Sciences, Surrey.

Dr Roger Searle   Marine geophysicist, Institute of Oceanographic Sciences, Surrey.

Laurence Draper   Marine physicist, Institute of Oceanographic Sciences, Surrey.

Dr Anthony S. Laughton   Marine geophysicist, Director, Institute of Oceanographic Sciences, Surrey.

Dr David Pugh   Marine physicist, Insitute of Oceanographic Sciences, Merseyside.

Dr Rupert Ormond   Marine Biologist, Lecturer at the University of York.

Brian Whitaker   Senior lecturer in geography, Sheffield City Polytechnic.

Robert L. Jack   Marine engineering consultant.

H. S. Noel   Journalist in fisheries and marine subjects.

Index

Picture acknowledgements

Aquila 42; Bruce Coleman 31, 39, 41; Bill Donohoe 8-9; Embassy of State of Bahrain 63; Embassy of State of Kuwait 50; Alan Gunstan 10; Alan Hutchison *front cover*, 6, 7, 19, 23, 25, 45, 47, 49, 53 (above), 58, 59, 60, 61, 62, 64; Institute of Oceanographic Sciences 16; Anna Jupp 11; John Mitchell 22; Dr. Ormond 20-21 (above), 27, 29, 30, 40, 65; Seaphot 38; The Weir Group 46; John Topham 13, 14, 15, 17, 52, 54, 55, 56; Vision International/ Pridgeon 36, 43; Wayland Picture Library 20-21 (below), 51, 53 (below), 57; Wood Hole Oceanographic Institute 12; World Health Organization 44; Zefa *title page*, 26, 28, 32, 33, 34, 35, 37, 48.